Toucan Play at This Game:

A Story of 100 Bird Puns & Play on Words

Produced by Andrew Weiss

Illustrated by Kathleen Darby

ACKNOWLEDGMENTS & DEDICATIONS

I want to make sure that 100 trillion thank yous are said to my wonderful family, friends and colleagues that helped inspire me to put this book together. Thank you for dealing with all my puns and snide remarks each day as well. Thank you to Shane Mileham for getting all this started with your random afternoon text challenging me with bird puns. Thank you to Jennifer Dodge and JD Studios for helping me find resources and giving me the inspiration to put 110% effort into all of it. Thank you to Kathleen Darby for creating all the awesome artwork! Thank you to my father Kurt Weiss for helping edit the book. Thank you to Shaun Tinney and Zeke Camusio and Brandon Zemp for your mentorship. Thank you to Yesenia Delgado for your help with the footnote idea. Thank you to Hannah Dodson for your help with the play format idea. I also want to thank Jules Son of Eris and Maya and Meeka for featuring me on their Facebook pages! Thank you to Steven Howsley for all the celebrity quote ideas. Thank you to Bryan Heathman with Made for Success Publishing for your guidance! The list goes on and on for all the appreciation I have. Also many thanks to whoever is reading this and may it be the funniest pun book you've read in your life so far!

FOREWORD

This book will help you in so many ways -- you'll laugh, you'll learn about birds, and you'll slowly start to question everything. To my knowledge, this book has more bird puns than any other book, which is an impressive feat considering bird puns are such a popular art form. It is most certainly worth a read, if only for the bragging rights that you're actively consuming the most bird puns you possibly can.

-Jo Firestone, Creator of Punderdome: A Card Game for Pun Lovers

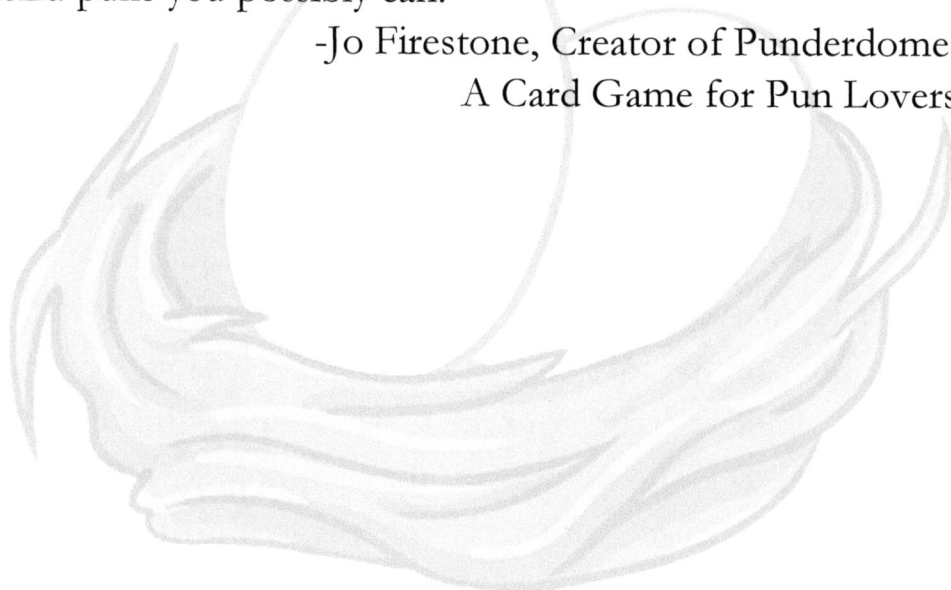

PREFACE

Growing up I used to hate the play on words that seemed pointless and desperate attempts to be funny. But over the past few years I have grown more fond of them as I've realized while they still may be cheap shots in the humor world, it's important to keep our brains active as far as viewing things from different points of view. So by using my social media app Snapchat I did a pun a day for about a year and a half. After reaching over 400 puns I just decided to say them in everyday conversations whether people appreciated them or not. My friends and family began to notice my increased use of puns and every time they saw or heard of one they'd send them my way or challenge me to a pun-off. A couple years ago I was challenged by my best friend when he led with a random text- "Want to exchange bird puns? Toucan play at this game." And the rest, we decided to wing it. There are 100 bird puns/malapropisms/play on words for you to enjoy. If Toucan play at this game, can you?

If you enjoy this book, tell your crushes, baes and fan clubs about it and follow us on Facebook, Instagram and Twitter at "Prestige Puns" for more punomenal words and phrases. Or send us an email at prestigepuns@gmail.com to join our community. Cheers!

It was a bright and sunny day in Southern California with a cold wind chill of 72 degrees.
Shane had spent years cleverly conniving a way to conquer his competitor until finally, it **CA-CAWLED**[1] to him. He had visited the local zoo and saw a Toucan.

SHANE
"Ah-hah! Let the games begin. (He then proceeded to text his lifelong friend and superior punmaster Andrew) Want to exchange bird puns? **TOUCAN**[2] play at this game."

Now, Andrew had an arsenal of creative thinking and quick decision-making to counter this attack on his skillsets. However, nobody knew the extensive time, commitment and groans that would arise from the greatest bird pun exchange the world has ever seen.

ANDREW
"Ah, but how do I know you won't be **ROBIN**[3] me of all my puns?"

"You let me rob you of your puns, and I'll let you **FLA-MINGLE**[4] with my girls."

Andrew strategically rested well that night. From writing many bird puns in advance, to cutting off Shanes network, he was willing to do anything and everything to be the BIRD PUN CHAMPION.

"That's great because we can **PARROT**[5] all together."

"Speaking of working together, how would a bunch of birds construct a building?"

"**CROW**fully?"[6]

And hopefully no one will **HAWK**[10] a loogie on the building."

"Did he just defend the double bird pun text with his own double bird pun text?"

Shane didn't respond for two months. They both secretly talked to the world's best ornithologists and flew around the world discovering new species, just to become the ultimate champion.

"Of course. But if caught and put behind bars, the jaywalkers could just leave through the **CONDOR**."[13]

"And when they're caught, how will the police know to pick between this-**SWAN**[14] and that one?"

"It depends on how **GULL**ible[15] the police are."

"Well, I'm glad they survived because my friend was hoping someone **WOOD-PECK-ER**[22] on the cheek to celebrate."

"Ooh that was a **FOWL**[23] joke."

"I'm glad you found it **EMU**sing."[24]

"Now you're looking them up. That's not going to **FLY**."[25]

"Yes I agree! Let **OSPREY**[33] I don't sprain my ankle from wearing bad shoes in the storm."

"Yeah, I hope it's not **MOA**[34] than you can handle."

"Sounds like you'll need **TWEET**ment[39] for that burn."

"It ruffles my **FEATHERS**."[40]

"You used those ones already! Yes, I'm being a **TATTLER**.[41] Since it's already taken...

"...That's **AUK**..."[42]

"Well that certainly wouldn't be **PHEASANT**."[48]

"Especially if you travel to **PHOENIX**,[49] Arizona."

"Ah but fishing with a stick or a spork? Or if both, a **STORK**."[52]

"**GEESE**,[53] that was a good pun."

"Thanks! Now it's your **TERN**."[54]

I would go but I'm still upset you ate **MAG-PIE**!"[55]

YOINK!

33

"Assuredly making them into a **LOON**-atic."[60]

"Well I still love them because each joke will **RHEAS**[61] the roof!"

"Hopefully no one does any **GROUSE**[69] acts while dancing to the music."

"I doubt it since it's orKESTREL[70] music."

"That's what you think, but I've set a **BOOBY**[78] trap!"

!!!

A Hard Place

"Can't think of a new one? I guess you're stuck between a **ROC**[79] and a hard place."

Andrew finally decided to give it all he had by pouring several more hours of research and sweat into winning this excessive exchange- regardless of repeats and losing his pride.

"Haha! Now stop causing such a **ROC**us."[79]

"I'm practically a **BEAK**on[82] of hope!"

"Ah yes! I'm sure everyone is happy to **QUAIL**come[83] you into their home."

"Yes, but they'll fine me if I get dirt on the carpet, and I don't want a **SHOEBILL**."[84]

"Oh! I don't think you'll have to worry un**TEAL**[85] that actually happens."

49

"Well I'll try not to hit people with a spoon so I don't risk a **SPOONBILL**[90] too."

"Yeah and if you hit their bill too much it will lead to a **GROSBEAK**."[91]

Ew!

Grosbeak

"Birds always make friends with Disney princesses, and I'm sure **ORIOLE**[92] would sing to a **GROSBEAK**."[91]

"Either way, the goal should always be **TOWHEE**n[93] over the girl."

"Then what'll you **DOWITCHER**?"[94]

"I'd **PIGEON**[95] money to her favorite charity!"

"And if you gave that money to a church she'd know for sure there was a **GODWIT**er."[96]

"Yeah and she can **BEAK**on[97] a new holy life."

Shane finally saw the light at the end of the tunnel and knew he could win. He finished Andrew off with several consecutive puns to reach 100. Those final puns were:

"That joke is one of my **fAVES**![97] Once we hit 100 puns we can stop and go play **FLETCH**[98] with the dog...

"Why did I agree to the iTunes terms and conditions?!"

We'll say 'CHICKADEEz[103] out!' and she'll love her new clothes...

"Who wants tickets to the gun show?!"

Afterwards, go home and watch the POULTRYgeist[104] together. While NESTling[105] up close. 100 bird puns!...

THE END

PUN GUIDE

1. Called
2. Two can
3. Robbing
4. Mingle
5. Pair it
6. Carefully
7. Construction crane
8. Swift, a.k.a fast
9. Spare (it's a stretch, I know)
10. Hawk is an old verb dating back to the late 16th century and associated with coughing something up
11. Jaywalker
12. Illegal
13. A con door a.k.a. an exit for cons in prison
14. This one or that one
15. Gullible
16. Dove a.k.a. quickly making a decision
17. Ill
18. Goes
19. Inch
20. Happen
21. Ducked. Should be obvious
22. Would peck her
23. Foul
24. Amusing
25. Not fly a.k.a not going to work
26. Winged it as in used some improvisation
27. Buzzer
28. Burden
29. Excellent
30. Next
31. Here on
32. Weather the storm, as in control it
33. Us prey
34. More
35. Swallow, as in gulp
36. Chicken or coward
37. Talented
38. Venture

39. Treatment

40. Ruffling feathers means causing someone to be annoyed or upset

41. Tattler as in someone who tattles

42. Auk is short for "awkward"

43. Rook bird. Rookie means first timer or begginner

44. Human

45. Bald eagle. Bald means not having any hair

46. Hedwig is the owl character from Harry Potter

47. Murder means both to kill and is also a group of crows

48. Pleasant

49. Phoenix is both a type of bird and city in Arizona

50. Rent it

51. Kingfisher as in "the best fisher"

52. Stork is a combination of a stick and a fork according to us

53. Jeez which is associated with being short for "Jesus"

54. Turn

55. My pie

56. Turkey is both a bird and a country in Europe

57. Mocking a.k.a. copying

58. Raving

59. Cuckoo can also mean crazy

60. Lunatic

61. Raise

62. Regrets

63. Short for awkward...again

64. Starting

65. A stretch

66. Pele, one of the greatest soccer players of all time

67. Relevant

68. Either

69. Gross

70. Orchestral

71. Squashed

72. Woodstock

73. Rushing

74. Stoked, a.k.a pumped

75. Pair of kittens

76. May call

77. Ready

78. Booby is both a word and a type of trap

79. Rock

80. Titillating as in exciting

81. Petroleum

82. Beacon

83. Welcome

84. Shoe bill

85. Until

86. Fall con, as in a con in the Fall

87. God with

88. Cop lover

89. Really

90. Getting billed because of spoons

91. Gross beak

92. Ariel

93. To win

94. Do with her

95. Pitch in

96. Begin

97. Favorites

98. Fetch

99. Birdie, an object used in the sport badminton

100. Budget

101. Slang term for woman

102. Foxy aka. sexy

103. Check these

104. Poltergeist

105. Nestling, as in snuggling

106. Great

107. Fledglings, as in beginners/inexperienced

108. Game is both a form of play and animals/birds to hunt

MEET THE CREATORS

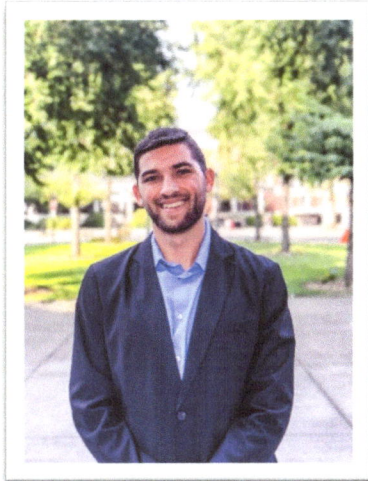

Andrew Weiss

Born under the wings of great punmasters before him, Andrew strives for greatness in the pun world. Residing in Oregon throughout his life, he started off his punmanship by using the platform Snapchat. Creating a pun a day, he reached over 400 puns within a couple years. You can follow him at Weissguy44. Constantly being sent puns and jokes from family and friends, his arsenal is constantly growing. In his free time outside of PUNishing people with his humor, he enjoys spending time with his cats Moose and Rocko, playing basketball and hiking outdoors.

Kathleen Darby

I study the world through drawing. As my most immediate output of my brain, sketches and diagrams pose as my most fluent form of communication. Drawing at two years old and using MS Paint at 3, I have been an artist for as long as I can remember. I thrive at the intersection of analogue and digital art making processes. I have graduated with a BFA in Digital Arts from the University of Oregon.

www.ingramcontent.com/pod-product-compliance
Lightning Source LLC
LaVergne TN
LVHW072111070426
835509LV00003B/115